Recipes from a

CAPE COD KITCHEN

The New England Book Co.

Portsmouth, NH 03802

1991

CONTENTS

Abbreviations

1 tsp.	1 teaspoon
1 tbsp	1 tablespoon
1 c.	1 cup
1 oz.	1 ounce
1 lb.	1 pound
1 pt.	1 pint
1 qt.	1 quart
B.P.	baking powder
R.I.	Rhode Island
*	editor's note

Ovens

quick	450º F
hot	400º F
medium	350º F
slow	300º F

This book is dedicated to James W. McCue, founder of The New England Book Company, who gathered the materials used in its preparation.

"Jim" was widely known throughout New England for his unaffected stories of Americana. His career started with writing for Boston newspapers in the 1930s and flourished in the 1950s with his short stories about New England. He believed in the power of the printed word to improve people's lives, and brought that belief to his work. His most cherished review was that of Boston newspaper columnist Neal O'Hara, who wrote of Jim in the 1940s - "...An ex-newspaperman who writes worthwhile stuff between cloth bound covers...".

This book is also dedicated to Alan Gore Lucas, who encouraged us to take on the project. Alan has always been an inspiration and a blessing to those who have known him.

**James W. McCue (front)
aboard a train at Edaville Railroad**

Carver (1940)

WEIGHTS AND MEASURES

	Pounds to bushel	Pounds to peck	Ounces to quart
Apples	48	12	24
Dried Apples	25	6 ¼	12 ½
Barley	48	12	24
Beans	60	15	30
Beans (Shell)	28	7	14
Beans (Soy)	58	14 ½	29
Beans (String)	24	6	12
Beets	60	15	30
Beet Greens	12	3	6
Bran & Shorts	20	5	10
Buckwheat	48	12	24
Carrots	50	12 ½	25
Corn, Cracked	50	12 ½	25
Corn, Indian	56	14	28
Cranberries	32	8	16
Dandelions	12	3	6
Meal (except Oat)	50	12 ½	25
Oats	32	8	16
Onions	52	13	26
Parsley	8	2	4
Parsnips	45	11 ¼	22 ½
Peaches	48	12	24
Pears	58	14 ½	29
Potatoes	60	15	30
Potatoes, Sweet	54	13 ½	27
Spinach	12	3	6
Tomatoes	56	14	28
Turnips	55	13 ¾	27 ½
Wheat	60	15	30

WEIGHTS AND MEASURES

1 quart sifted flour weighs 1 pound.

1 quart Indian meal weighs 1 pound 2 ounces.

1 quart powdered sugar weighs 1 pound 1 ounce.

1 quart granulated sugar weighs 1 pound 9 ounces.

1 quart best brown sugar weighs 1 pound 2 ounces.

1 quart soft butter weighs 1 pound 1 ounce.

1 pint closely packed butter weighs 1 pound.

Butter size of an egg equals ¼ cup and weighs 2 ounces.

10 eggs average 1 pound.

2 tablespoons of liquid weighs 1 ounce.

4 teaspoons of liquid equals 1 tablespoon.

3 teaspoons of dry material equal 1 tablespoon.

4 tablespoon of liquid equals 1 wine glass, ½ gill, or ¼ cup.

16 tablespoon of liquid equals 1 cup.

8 heaping tablespoons of dry material equals 1 cup.

2 gills equals 1 cup or ½ pint.

4 cups of liquid equals 1 quart.

1 pint of milk or water equals 1 pound.

1 pint chopped meat solidly packed equals 1 pound.

A pinch of salt or spice is about a saltspoonful.

CAPE COD IN SEPTEMBER

Come with me in September
When the beach plum is full,
With fruit and color,
It is something to remember.

Come with me in September
When autumn paints,
With yellow, brown and gold,
Its glorious splendour.

Come with me in September
When life is still,
With peace and grace,
Its spirit yet a glowing ember.

Come with me,
To Cape Cod in September.

JWM

Eastham (1938)

Provincetown (1935)

YEAST BREADS and ROLLS

WHITE BREAD

2 tsp. salt

2 tbsp. sugar

1 tbsp. butter

2 c. scalded milk*

1 c. lukewarm water with

1 yeast cake dissolved

Add scalded milk to sugar, salt, butter and lard and let stand until lukewarm. Then add mixture of water and yeast cake. Stir into this mixture 8 c. of flour which has not been sifted. Beat until mixture is well blended. Let rise until light. Knead and put into tins. This mixture makes 2 big loaves and a small pan of biscuits. When well risen bake about 45 minutes in medium oven. *A teaspoon of baking soda may be added to the scalded milk and the salt eliminated, if desired.

INDIAN BREAD

1 c. Indian Meal*

¼ c. shortening

¼ c. molasses

½ yeast cake

2 c. boiling water

1 pinch salt

¼ c. sugar

Scald meal in boiling water and mix in other ingredients. Add in enough white flour to allow the mixture to be kneaded. Allow to rise as with white bread. Bake in medium oven for about 45 minutes. *Coursely milled corn meal.

CINNAMON ROLLS

¼ c. sugar
½ tsp. salt
¼ c. butter

1 c. scalded milk
1 yeast cake
1 egg beaten slightly

Mix ingredients together and blend well. Add enough white flour to the mixture to make a soft dough. Knead and let rise for about 3 hours. Roll dough out to ½ inch thickness, spread generously with melted butter and a mixture of sugar, cinnamon and seedless raisins. Roll up like jelly roll, cut off slices ¾ inch thick, place close together in pan. Let rise again and bake in hot oven. Spread with confectioner's frosting as soon as taken from oven.

QUICK BISCUITS

1 tsp. sugar
1 tsp. butter
¼ tsp. salt

½ c. warm milk
1 yeast cake
1 c. flour

Dissolve yeast cake in warm milk with sugar and butter. Sift flour and salt, mix and form into ball using more flour if necessary. Cover and let rise nearly ½ hour in warm place. Roll to ½ inch thickness, cut into biscuit; let rise in pan about ½ hour over a dish of hot water. Bake in a hot oven.

NUT BREAD

¼ yeast cake
½ c. lukewarm water
1 tbsp. shortening
1 c. chopped walnut

1 c. scalded milk
3 tbsp. molasses
1 tsp. salt
½ c. entire wheat flour*

Mix shortening and scalded milk, allow to cool to room temperature. Dissolve yeast cake in warm water and add salt, molasses and chopped walnut. Blend the water and milk mixtures together and slowly add the wheat flour. Mix well and add white flour as needed to form a dough. Knead and allow to rise. Knead once again and place in tin. Allow to rise again, and bake medium oven for about 45 minutes. *Entire wheat flour is course milled whole wheat flour, regular whole wheat flour may be used.

PARKER HOUSE ROLLS

½ tbsp. lard
1 tbsp. butter
1 egg
½ tsp. salt

1 can evaporated milk
2 yeast cakes
2 tbsp. sugar

Empty evaporated milk and fill can twice with water, add to milk and scald. Mix with dry ingredients and let stand until lukewarm. Dissolve yeast cakes in ½ c. lukewarm water, combine mixtures and add enough flour to make a very soft batter. Let stand until full of bubbles (about 1 hour). Add a well beaten egg to the batter and mix well. Now add enough flour to form a dough, being careful not to get the dough too hard or stiff. Cover and let rise until the dough is light. Cut down and roll the dough to about ½ inch thickness and cut out rounds. Butter and fold the rounds on a well greased pan and let rise until double in size. Bake in hot oven until tops are golden. Brush tops with butter while still hot.

SCOTCH BUNS

2 c. milk
½ yeast cake
½ c. water
1 egg

1 tsp. salt
¾ c. sugar
⅓ c. butter

Scald milk, dissolve yeast cake in water. Cream sugar, butter and egg. When milk is cool, pour in sugar, butter and egg mixture and add salt. Now add enough bread flour to make a stiff batter, do not knead. Let the batter rise over night, then roll out to about ½ inch thick and spread well with butter, brown sugar, small seedless raisins and cinnamon. Roll up as for jelly cake, cut in ½ wide slices, place in greased pan and allow to rise for 2 hours. Bake in hot oven until golden. While still hot, glaze tops with powdered sugar and water.

CORN BREAD

1 qt. milk
1 tsp. salt
½ yeast cake
2 eggs

1 pt. corn meal
1 tbsp. butter
½ c. white flour
½ tsp. baking soda

Scald the milk and mix with the corn meal, flour and butter. After the mixture has cooled to room temperature, mix in salt and yeast dissolved in ½ c. lukewarm water. Allow mixture to stand overnight at room temperature. Then add eggs (well beaten) and baking soda (dissolved in tbsp. warm water), and mix well. Pour mixture into buttered tins, let rise, and bake in hot oven for about 30 minutes.

QUICK BREADS and MUFFINS

BOSTON BROWN BREAD

1 c. rye meal
1 c. corn meal
2 c. sour milk
¾ tsp. baking soda

¾ c. molasses
1 c. graham flour
2 tsp. salt

Mix and sift dry ingredients, add molasses and milk and stir well. Place in a well buttered tin and cook slowly. If baked (2 hours) it has the consistency of bread. If steamed (4 hours) it has the constancy of cake.

POP OVERS

2 c. flour
2 c. milk

3 eggs
1 tsp. salt

Beat eggs until light, add salt and milk, turn slowly into sifted flour, beating briskly all the time. Heat gem pans, grease and half fill with batter. Bake in hot oven 20 minutes without disturbing.

EGG MUFFINS

2 tbsp. melted butter
2 eggs
½ c. sugar
1 c. milk

2 c. bread flour
1 tsp. cream of tartar
½ tsp. baking soda
½ tsp. salt

Beat eggs thoroughly and blend in melted butter, sugar and milk. Sift together flour, cream of tartar, baking soda and salt, and slowly blend into the liquid mixture. Bake in hot oven for 20 minutes in well greased muffin tins.

BAKING POWDER BISCUITS

2 c. flour
4 tsp. B.P.
¾ c. milk

½ tsp. salt
2 tbsp. butter
2 tbsp. sugar*

Mix dry ingredients and sift several times. Work in butter and gradually add the liquid to make a soft dough. Roll lightly on floured board to ½ inch thickness and shape with biscuit cutter. Bake in hot oven for 12 to 15 minutes on a well buttered pan. * May be added if a dessert biscuit is desired.

YORKSHIRE PUDDING

3 c. bread flour
6 eggs

⅔ qt. milk
1 tsp. salt

Beat eggs, add milk, and mix well with flour and salt. Bake ¾ hour in shallow pan in hot oven.

SOUR MILK BREAD

2 c. flour
2 tbsp. shortening
½ c. brown sugar
2 c. sour milk

1 tsp. baking soda
2 c. bran or graham flour
1 c. raisins or chopped nuts
¼ tsp. salt

Sift flour together with salt and baking soda, and mix well with other dry ingredients. Melt shortening and mix with sour milk. Slowly blend liquid and dry mixtures together, and bake in a well greased loaf pan in a moderate oven until brown.

CORN BREAD

¾ c. sugar
1 tsp. butter
1 tsp. lard
1 egg
½ tsp baking soda

1 tsp. cream of tartar
1 c. milk
1 c. flour
1 c. corn meal

Mix all dry ingredients together. Mix milk with melted butter, melted lard, and well beaten egg. Slowly blend liquid and dry ingredients together and mix well. Pour into a well greased tin and cook in hot oven until golden brown.

PEANUT BUTTER BREAD

2 c. flour
2 tsp. B.P.
¾ tsp. salt
2 eggs

½ c. sugar
1 c. peanut butter
1 c. milk

Sift together dry ingredients and cut the peanut butter into these as you would lard into biscuit ingredients. Add beaten eggs with milk and mix well. Bake at once in greased tin in a moderate oven.

GRAHAM BREAD

2 c. sour milk
¼ c. sugar
¼ c. molasses
½ c. walnut meat

3 ½ c. sifted graham flour
1 tsp. baking soda
2 tsp. baking powder

Sift together flour, baking soda and baking powder. Mix in crushed walnut meat and sugar. Blend well with molasses. Add sour milk slowly and mix well. Place in well buttered tin and bake 1 hour in moderate oven.

RAISIN BREAD

1 c. sugar
1 egg
4 c. flour
1 c. walnuts

1 c. raisins
4 tsp. B.P.
1 ½ c. milk

Mix all ingredients together and allow to stand in a warm place for 2 hours. Place in a well greased pan and bake for 1 hour in moderate oven.

PANCAKES

1 c. flour
1 c. corn meal
¼ c. sugar
1 tsp. B.P.

2 eggs
1 tbsp. melted butter
1 c. milk

Mix dry ingredients together and then add milk and eggs. Fold all ingredients together gently until mixed and then beat 5 minutes. Cook immediately on a well greased hot grill. Batter may also be baked in a shallow pan, this will give you a very pleasant "Johnny Cake".

BREAD GRIDDLE CAKES

1 c. flour
3 c. scalded milk
2 eggs
4 tbsp. butter

2 c. stale bread crumbs
8 tsp. B.P.
½ tsp. salt

Add milk and butter to finely broken bread crumbs and allowed to soak until soft. Mix and sift together flour, salt and B.P., and added to milk mixture. Beat thoroughly each time before cooking on a well greased, hot grill. When puffed full of bubbles and cooked at the edges, turn and cook on the other side. Serve hot.

BUCKWHEAT CAKES

4 c. tepid water
3 tbsp. molasses (not self-rising)
½ cake yeast
1 tsp. salt

4 c. buckwheat

¼ tsp. baking soda

Set buckwheat, water, yeast and salt in large pitcher over night. In the morning add molasses and baking soda (dissolved in tbsp. hot water) to pitcher and mix well. Cook on a well greased, hot griddle.

HUCKLEBERRY PANCAKES

2 c. R.I. corn meal   2 tbsp. sugar
1 tsp. salt boiling water

Pour over the dry ingredients enough boiling water to make a stiff dough. Beat the dough hard and cover it for 15 minutes. Thin the dough with cold milk so it will drop from a spoon in thick small cakes on griddle. Add 2 c. huckleberries, which have been rolled in flour, to the batter before cooking. Cook on a hot, well greased griddle. Josselyn, writing in 1639, said that "the English made a standard dish of boyled meal and hucleberries". *(white corn meal)

WAFFLES

2 c. flour   ½ tsp. salt
3 egg yolks   2 c. cream
2 tsp B.P   2 ¼ tsp. powdered sugar
3 egg whites   1 tsp. melted butter

Mix dry ingredients together and blend in a mixture of egg yolks, cream and melted butter. Mix well and then fold in well beaten egg whites. Cook on a well heated and greased waffle iron.

ORANGE TEA BISCUITS

4 c. flour   3 tbsp. shortening
5 tsp. B.P. (half butter and lard)
2 tbsp. sugar   1 ½ tsp salt
1 egg   2 tbsp. grated orange rind
2 ½ c. milk

Sift together all dry ingredients, and beat together milk, shortening and egg. Fold dry ingredients into milk mixture and grated rind. Bake on a lightly greased cookie sheet in hot oven until tops just begin to brown.

FRUIT GEMS

2 eggs
1 c. milk
1 tsp. B.P.

1 ½ c. graham flour
1 c. white flour
1 c. chopped dates and figs

Mix yolks of eggs and milk, fold in flour and B.P. (sifted together) and chopped fruits. Mix well and then fold in stiffly beaten egg whites. Bake in well greased muffin tin for about 20 minutes in a medium oven.

CRANBERRY MUFFINS

½ c. butter
¼ c. sugar
1 egg
¾ c. milk

1 c. cranberries
2 c. sifted bread flour
2 tsp. B.P.
½ tsp. salt

Cream butter and sugar, add well beaten egg and milk. Fold in flour, B.P. and salt after sifting together. Mix well and fold in cranberries after they have been cut in halves. Bake in well buttered muffin tins in a moderate oven.

CORN MEAL MUFFINS

1 egg
¾ c. sugar
1 c. wheat flour
1 pinch salt

2 tsp. B.P.
1 c. corn meal
1 c. milk

Take 1 c. unsifted flour and sift together with other dry ingredients. Mix egg and milk well and slowly add to dry ingredients. Mix well and place in a well buttered muffin tin. Cook in medium oven until golden brown on top.

OATMEAL MUFFINS

2 c. rolled oats
1 ½ c. sour milk
2 tbsp. melted butter
3 tbsp. sugar

1 egg
1 tsp. baking soda
½ tsp. salt
1 c. pastry flour

Soak rolled oats in the sour milk for 2 hours, and then add a well beaten egg to this mixture. Sift remaining dry ingredients together and fold into the milk mixture. Mix well and fill (to ⅔) well buttered muffin tins. Bake in hot oven until brown.

BRAN MUFFINS

1 c. bran
1 c. white flour
1 c. graham flour
1 c. sweet milk

¼ tsp. salt
⅓ c. molasses
1 tsp. baking soda
½ c. currants or raisins

¼ c. hot water

Sift dry ingredients together. Mix molasses and hot water and blend into milk. Fold dry mixture into liquid and mix well. Bake in moderate oven in well greased muffin tins.

Main Street in Plymouth (1946)

Currier's can be seen in the front left of the photo. Harold Currier and his wife ran this most distinctive and loved restaurant from the 1930s to the 1960s. Their Indian pudding and blueberry muffins were a delight to residents and visitors alike.

DESSERTS

OLD FASHIONED INDIAN PUDDING

1 c. corn meal	2 ½ qts. milk
4 eggs	1 ½ c. dark molasses
1 c. sugar	3 tbsp. butter
2 tsp. salt	2 tsp. cinnamon
1 tsp. ginger	

Scald 1 qt. milk. Add 1 c. corn meal,stirring constantly and cooking until slightly thickened. Beat 4 eggs, add sugar, salt, cinnamon, ginger and molasses. Add to corn meal mixture and stir well. Pour into buttered earthenware baking dish and stir in 1 qt. cold milk. Dot with butter and bake in low oven for 2 hours. Add 1 pt. cold milk, without stirring, and return to low oven and cook for several more hours. The longer it is cooked the more firm the pudding becomes. Do not let it dry out. Serve hot or cold with heavy cream, whipped cream or vanilla ice cream.

This is a generous sized pudding especially suitable for holiday occasions and family gatherings. The recipe given here was featured at Currier's in Plymouth for more than 30 years.

INDIAN TAPIOCA PUDDING

⅓ c. tapioca	¼ c. indian meal*
1 c. molasses	4 c. milk
1 tsp. butter	1 pinch salt

Cook tapioca, meal and milk in a double boiler until the cereals are soft and have thickened the milk. Add the molasses, butter and salt. Cook for 2 hours in a moderate oven. *Coarsely ground corn meal.

RICE PUDDING

1 qt. milk
1 qt. water
1 pinch salt

½ c. rice
½ c. molasses

Boil rice in water, drain and wash. Add milk, molasses and salt, and mix well. Bake in a well buttered covered dish for 7 hours, remove cover during the last ½ hour to allow top to slightly brown. During baking add milk if necessary to keep moist.

STEAMED DATE PUDDING

½ c. molasses
½ c. milk
1 ⅔ c. flour
3 tbsp. melted butter
½ lb. stoned dates

½ tsp. baking soda
¼ tsp. salt
¼ tsp. clove
¼ tsp. allspice
¼ tsp. nutmeg

Shift together flour, salt, baking soda, and spices. Mix butter and milk, and fold in flour mixture. Add molasses and mix thoroughly. Fold in stoned (or thinly sliced) dates. Place in lightly buttered pan and steam for 2 ½ hours. Serve hot with cold cream or vanilla ice cream.

BREAD PUDDING

1 pt. milk
1 c. bread crumbs
1 tbsp. butter

3 egg yolks
1 grated lemon rind
1 c. sugar*

Scald milk and pour over bread crumbs and butter. When cool, add beaten egg yolks, lemon rind and sugar. Mix gently and pour into a shallow, buttered dish and bake lightly. * ½ c. of sugar may be used if you prefer it less sweet. If you like it sweeter, make a mixture of lemon juice and sugar for the top and bake until lightly brown.

COTTAGE PUDDING

1 c. flour	1 tsp. B.P.
½ c. sugar	1 tbsp. melted butter
1 c. milk	1 egg

Sift together flour, sugar and B.P., and add this to a mixture of well beaten milk, egg and melted butter. Mix well and bake in lightly buttered muffin tins in hot oven. Don't let them burn! While these are cooking make a sauce for them by boiling a mixture of 1 c. flour (which is added slowly to 1 c. cold water), ¾ c. sugar, 2 tbsp. melted butter, and ½ tsp vanilla. When the mixture has boiled to sufficient thickness allow to cool slightly before use on the Cottage Pudding.

Cottage pudding was a staple of Cape Cod winters. Although simple in ingredients, it makes an enjoyable dessert and can be made elegant with fresh blueberries or vine ripened strawberries on the top.

APPLE ROLL

4 apples	1 pt. water
1 ½ c. sugar	1 piece butter
cinnamon	

Select apples that will cook quickly, peel, core, and chop fine. Put sugar and water in baking pan over low heat. While syrup is cooking slowly, make a rich biscuit dough (see baking powder biscuit recipe). Roll out dough to about ½ thick, spread with chopped apples and roll into a long roll. Make cuts in roll about 1 ½ inches apart, and place cut side down in hot syrup. Put a small piece of butter on top and sprinkle with cinnamon and sugar. Bake in a hot oven until apples are cooked and crust is golden. Turn out on a platter and pour syrup around it. Serve plain or topped with whipped cream.

CRANBERRY PUDDING

1 c. sugar
3 tsp. butter
1 c. milk
1 ½ c. cranberries

2 c. flour
2 tsp. cream of tartar
1 tsp. baking soda

Cream sugar and butter, add milk, and slowly blend in flour, cream of tartar and baking soda (previously sifted together). Fold in whole cranberries, and bake ½ hour in moderate oven.

Serve with lemon sauce (lemon juice and sugar thickened by boiling) if desired.

CORN PUDDING

1 tbsp. sugar
2 eggs
rich milk

3 ears fresh, sweet corn
1 pinch salt

Grate several ears of fresh, sweet corn and mix with 2 well beaten eggs. Thin with a little rich milk. Add salt and sugar, and pour into buttered, shallow pie plates. Dot with butter and cook in moderate oven until crisp on edges and brown on top.

THANKSGIVING PUDDING

10 crackers
1 pt. raisins
1 c. suet
2 c. sugar

1 tsp. nutmeg*
4 eggs
3 pts. milk

Place in a pudding dish a layer of rolled crackers, raisins and suet. Pour over this 1 ½ pts milk and let stand over night. In the morning add sugar, beaten eggs, spices and remainder of milk. Cover and cook for 6 hours in slow oven. * Other spices may be used.

PLUM PUDDING

1 egg
½ c. molasses
1 tsp. cinnamon
½ tsp. clove
¼ tsp. nutmeg
1 tsp. baking soda

1 pt. flour
1 c. seedless raisins
1 c. currants
1 c. chopped suet
1 tsp. salt
1 c. sweet milk

Shift together flour, spices, salt and baking soda. Beat egg into milk, and slowly fold in the flour mixture. Now fold in molasses, raisins, currants and suet. Mix well and steam for 3 hours in a double boiler.

APRICOT PUDDING

24 apricots
gelatin
½ c. water
½ c. sugar
¼ tsp. salt

1 c. sugar
1 juice of lemon
1 pt. milk
3 egg yolks
1 tsp. corn starch

Soak apricots over night and cook until soft. Dissolve 1 envelope of gelatin in water and add the hot apricots with water they were cooked in. Add lemon juice and 1 c. sugar. Stir thoroughly and let harden. Make a custard for the top by mixing 3 well beaten egg yolks with 1 pt. of scalded milk, ½ c. sugar, ¼ tsp. salt, 1 tsp. corn starch and tbsp lemon juice. Simmer for 5 minutes, allow to cool and pour over gelatin mixture before custard sets. Serve when cooled. 12 peaches or 6 pears may be used in place of 24 apricots.

JUDGE PETERS PUDDING

2 c. boiling water
gelatin
1 c. cold water
2 bananas
6 figs

2 c. sugar
2 juice of lemons
2 oranges
10 dates
10 walnuts

Dissolve 2 pkgs. of gelatin in boiling water, add cold water, sugar and juice of lemons. When cool, add oranges, bananas, dates, figs and walnut meats, all cut in small pieces. Chill on ice.

PINEAPPLE PUDDING

2 tbsp. gelatin
1 pt. boiling water
½ pt. cream

1 c. sugar
4 egg whites
1 pt. sliced pineapple

Dissolve the gelatin in boiling water, add sugar and let stand until cold. Take the whites of eggs and beat stiff as possible, add to gelatin and beat until stiff and white. Whip the cream and stir into gelatin. Add pineapple (cut in small pieces) without juice, and set aside to harden. Best made a day or more before serving.

BUTTER SCOTCH PUDDING

¼ tsp. salt
¾ c. brown sugar
1 tsp. vanilla

1 ½ c. bread cubes
1 pt. scalded milk
2 eggs

Butter the bread and cut in cubes. Scald milk and let stand until bread is soft. Beat yolks, add salt and ½ c. brown sugar. Pour this over bread and milk mixture. Beat whites with remaining brown sugar for frosting with vanilla. Bake in buttered dish in slow oven.

BROWN SUGAR PUDDING

1 ½ c. brown sugar
2 c. hot water
3 egg whites

⅓ c. cornstarch
¼ c. cold water
½ c. nut meats

Cook brown sugar and hot water a few minutes in double boiler, add cornstarch which has been wet with the cold water. Stir until it thickens. Let cook about 20 minutes, take from fire, add beaten egg whites and nut meats. Serve with custard or cream.

DATE PUDDING

1 ½ c. sugar   1 pkg. dates
¾ c. butter   1 ½ c. sweet milk
3 eggs   1 c. walnut meat
1 ½ tbsp. flour   1 tsp. B.P.

Cream sugar, butter and eggs. Add milk, dates (cut up), walnut meat, B.P. and flour. Bake in slow oven until brown (about 1 ½ hours). Serve warm with whipped cream.

PUDDING SAUCE

1 egg white   1 c. powdered sugar
3 tsp. butter   1 tsp. vanilla

Mix all ingredients together and beat to a cream. May be made with ripened fruit puree in place of vanilla.

LEMON BREAD PUDDING

1 c. bread   2 egg yolks
1 pt. hot milk   1 piece butter
½ c. sugar   1 grated lemon peel
2 egg whites   1 c. sugar
1 juice of lemon

Mix hot milk, egg yolks, butter, ½ c. sugar and lemon peel. Pour over soft bread broken in small pieces in the bottom of baking dish. Bake slowly until set. Allow to cool to near room temperature and cover with a meringue of egg whites, ½ c. sugar and lemon juice that has been whipped stiff. Place pudding with meringue back in oven until to has begun to brown. Serve warm or cold.

FUDGE

2 c. sugar
2 sq. chocolate
1 piece butter

⅔ c. milk
⅛ tsp. salt

Slowly melt grated chocolate and butter in a double boiler, add sugar and continue to heat on open flame until all has melted. Fold in milk and continue to cook slowly on double boiler with frequent stirring for the better part of a day. Add small amounts of milk as needed to keep it a soft paste. Remove from heat and allow to cool in 1 inch deep pan.

ORANGE CAKE

1 c. sugar
½ c. butter
½ c. orange juice

1 c. flour
1 tsp. B.P.
2 eggs

Beat eggs thoroughly, add sugar, beating again thoroughly, add butter. Sift flour 3 times with B.P. and add, alternating with orange juice, to egg mixture. Bake in shallow cake pan for about 40 minutes in medium oven. Cover with frosting made from white of 1 egg, 1 c. powdered sugar and grated rind of ½ orange beaten to a stiff consistency.

CREAM SPONGE CAKE

4 egg yolks
1 c. sugar flour
1 ¼ tsp. B.P.
¼ tsp. salt

1 ½ tbsp. cornstarch
3 tbsp. cold water
4 egg whites
1 tsp. lemon extract

Beat yolks and water, add sugar gradually and beat 2 minutes. Put cornstarch in cup and fill with sifted flour and B.P., add to first mixture. When thoroughly mixed, add stiffly beaten egg whites and lemon extract. Bake in moderate oven for 30 to 40 minutes.

AFTERNOON TEA CAKES

1 tbsp. butter
1 c. sugar
2 egg yolks
1 c. sour cream
   flavoring

2 c. flour
1 tsp. B.P.
1 tsp. baking soda
2 egg whites

Cream butter, add sugar and well beaten yolks. Add cream and flour mixed with baking soda and baking powder. Add stiffly beaten egg whites and flavoring. Among favorite flavorings are vanilla, lemon, almond, rum and orange extract. Bake in gem pans in moderate oven. Batter may also be used for a layer cake.

POUND CAKE

1 ½ c. sugar
1 c. butter
4 eggs
1 ½ c. sifted flour

½ tsp. baking soda
¼ tsp. salt
4 tbsp. milk
1 tsp. vanilla

Cream butter and sugar, add egg yolks, beat well, add flour, baking soda and salt, then milk and last fold in the beaten whites, bake 1 hour in slow oven. Nuts, cherries or raisins may be added if desired.

ECONOMY CAKE

1 c. molasses
1 tbsp. melted butter
1 tsp. baking soda
1 c. raisins
1 ½ c. flour

⅔ c. warm water
1 pinch ground clove
1 pinch ground cinnamon
1 pinch grated nutmeg

Sift dry ingredients together. Mix molasses, warm water and melted butter together. Blend dry ingredients into water mixture. Bake in well buttered pan in slow oven.

HUCKLEBERRY CAKE

½ c. milk
2 c. bread flour
1 tsp. B.P.
2 c. huckleberries

1 tbsp. butter
1 ½ c. sugar
2 eggs

Cream butter and sugar together and add milk with beaten eggs. Fold together and slowly add flour sifted together with B.P., fold in huckleberries. Bake in slow oven.

SALT PORK CAKE

½ lb. salt pork
½ lb. brown sugar
½ c. molasses
4 c. flour
1 tsp. baking soda
1.2 tsp. cloves

1 ½ c. hot water
½ tsp. ginger
½ lb. seedless raisins
1 c. walnut meat
1 tsp. cinnamon

Pour hot water over salt pork and let stand until cold. Mix brown sugar, molasses, ginger, cinnamon, walnut meat and raisins. Add to salt pork and water. Fold into this mixture flour and baking soda after sifting. Mix well and bake in a slow oven until brown.

SWAMPSCOTT CAKE

1 ½ c. sugar
3 eggs
2 c. flour
1 tsp. vanilla
½ c. butter

2 tsp. warm water
½ tsp. baking soda
⅔ c. milk
½ tsp. salt

Cream sugar and butter, add egg yolks well beaten. Add milk and flour alternately. Dissolve baking soda in warm water and add 1 tsp. to cake mixture, stirring thoroughly. Add salt and vanilla. Fold in the stiffly beaten egg whites. Bake in a moderate oven for 1 hour in a tube pan.

UNION CAKE

2 c. sugar
½ c. butter
4 eggs
½ c. cornstarch

1 c. milk
2 ½ c. flour
2 tsp. yeast powder

Dissolve sugar and yeast powder in milk. Add well beaten eggs and butter to milk. Sift together cornstarch and flour , and fold slowly into milk mixture. Bake in medium oven.

SOUR MILK CAKE

1 c. sugar
2 tsp. coco
½ tsp. cinnamon
¼ tsp. ginger
¼ tsp nutmeg
⅛ tsp. clove

½ c. butter
1 tsp. baking soda
1 c. sour milk
2 c. bread flour
1 c. raisins
1 pinch salt

Mix sugar, coco, cinnamon, ginger, nutmeg, clove and salt and cream this mixture with butter. Add soda beaten into sour milk, sifted bread flour and raisins. Bake in slow oven.

COFFEE FRUIT CAKE

2 c. brown sugar
1 c. butter
1 c. molasses
½ tsp. B.P.
1 tsp. baking soda
½ tsp. salt
1 lb. currants

1 c. strong coffee
4 eggs
4 c. flour
1 tsp. cloves
1 tsp. nutmeg
1 lb. raisins
2 tsp. cinnamon

Mix flour, spices, B.P., salt, currants and raisins. Cream brown sugar, butter, molasses and well beaten eggs, and add coffee with continuous mixing. Blend flour mixture into this second mixture, and mix thoroughly. Bake in slow oven for several hours.

APPLE SAUCE CAKE

1 c. sugar
½ tsp. cloves
½ c. shortening
1 ¾ c. flour
1 tsp. baking soda

¼ tsp. nutmeg
1 c. sour apple sauce
1 tsp. cinnamon
1 c. raisins

Cream the shortening, sugar and spices. Dissolve the soda in a little hot water and stir into apple sauce. Add to the rest. Beat thoroughly and add flour and raisins. Bake about 45 minutes in hot oven.

CHRISTMAS CAKE

1 c. molasses
½ c. milk
1 egg
½ tsp. clove
½ tsp. nutmeg
1 tsp. baking soda

½ c. butter
½ c. sugar
1 c. chopped raisins
½ tsp. cinnamon
½ tsp ginger
1 pinch salt

Cream butter in sugar, add molasses and spices and mix. Add raisins and mix. Beat egg in milk and add to sugar mixture and blend thoroughly. Slowly add flour to entire mixture until a soft gingerbread consistency is obtained. Place in a well greased pan and bake quickly.

SLICED APPLE CAKE

2 c. flour
2 tsp. B.P.
½ c. sugar
1 pinch salt

1 egg
1 tbsp. butter
½ c. milk

Cream butter and sugar and mix with milk. Sift flour, B.P. and salt together and fold into milk mixture. Cover thickly with sweet, sliced apples. Bake in medium oven. Serve with shipped cream flavored with almond extract.

SOUR MILK DOUGHNUTS

1 c. sugar
1 egg
1 tsp. nutmeg
1 tsp. cinnamon
  flour

1 c. sour milk
1 tsp. baking soda
1 tsp. baking soda
1 tbsp. melted lard

Mix egg and melted lard together and add milk (should be soured to the point of jelling). Add sugar, spices and baking soda. Mix well. Fold in flour until the dough can be handled and cut (not too stiff). Cook in very hot lard until brown.

OATMEAL COOKIES

1 c. shortening
1 c. sugar
2 eggs
5 tbsp. milk
½ tsp. salt
1 tsp. baking soda
flour

¼ tsp. clove
¼ tsp. cinnamon
¼ tsp. nutmeg
¼ tsp. ginger
2 c. rolled oats
1 c. raisins

Cream sugar, shortening and eggs together and add spices, baking soda, milk and oats. Mix well and add just enough sifted flour to bind together. Drop from spoon on to greased pans and cook in moderate oven until golden brown.

HERMITS

1 c. sugar
¼ c. butter
¼ c. lard
1 egg
1 ½ c. flour
½ c. sour milk

½ tsp. baking soda
1 c. chopped raisins
1 tsp. cinnamon
½ c. sour milk
½ tsp. clove
½ tsp. nutmeg and allspice

Cream butter, lard, sugar and egg. Add spices and raisins and mix well. Add sour milk and mix until sugar dissolves. Blend in flour after shifting. Roll out and cut to shape. Bake in hot oven until brown.

HERMITS

1 c. butter
1 ½ c. brown sugar
1 tsp. baking soda
½ tsp. cloves
flour

3 eggs
1 tsp. cinnamon
½ c. sour milk
½ tsp. nutmeg

Prepare as above.

BROWNIES

2 eggs
½ c. flour
1 c. sugar
1 tsp. vanilla

1 c. walnuts
2 sqs. chocolate
½ c. butter

Beat eggs well, mix flour with sugar and eggs. Melt chocolate with butter and add to mixture. Add vanilla and walnuts. Blend well and place in cake pan. Bake 15 minutes in a quick oven.

FILLED COOKIES

1 c. sugar
½ c. shortening
1 egg
½ c. sugar
½ c. hot water

½ c. milk
2 tsp. B.P.
3 c. flour
1 tbsp. flour
1 c. chopped raisins

Mix 1 c. sugar, ½ c. shortening, 1 egg, and ½ c. milk. Slowly blend in flour sifted with B.P. and let stand over night.

Make a filing from ½ c. of sugar dissolved in ½ c. hot water and 1 c. of chopped raisins. To this add 1 tbsp. of flour and let stand over night. The next day roll out the cookie dough, cut and spread ½ of the cuts with filing and cover with the other cuts. Press edges together and cook in a hot oven until golden.

BOSTON COOKIES

1 c. butter	1 tbsp. baking soda
1 ½ c. sugar	1 ½ tbsp. hot water
3 eggs	3 ¼ c. flour
½ tsp. salt	1 tsp. cinnamon
1 c. walnut meat	1 c. raisins

Cream butter, sugar, eggs (well beaten), salt, baking soda, and cinnamon. Add hot water to make a paste and fold in nuts and raisins. Fold in shifted flour to form a buttery batter that will drop from a spoon. Bake in hot oven on buttered tins.

OATMEAL COOKIES

1 c. sugar	2 eggs
2 c. flour	⅔ c. lard
2 c. oatmeal	1 tsp. vanilla
1 tsp. baking soda	½ c. raisins
1 pinch salt	

Mix together dry ingredients. Slowly mix in lard. Mix thoroughly and then mix in eggs. Drop from spoon on to buttered tin and bake in hot oven until brown.

MOLASSES COOKIES

1 c. molasses	1 tsp. baking soda
½ c. lard	2 ½ c. flour
½ c. cold water	1 pinch salt

Mix molasses, lard and water together. Add baking soda dissolved in a tbsp. hot water, and salt. Fold in flour to make a dough that can be dropped from a spoon. Bake on greased tin in quick oven.

SCOTCH SHORT BREAD

1 c. butter	2 c. flour
½ c. brown sugar	

Cream butter, and flour, then sugar. Chill before rolling out thin. Bake in hot oven.

Picking cranberries on Cape Cod (1921)

Before the introduction of automated equipment all work on the bogs was done by hand. From weeding in spring and summer to picking in the fall, the work was hard.

GINGER BREAD

1 tsp. ginger
1 tsp. baking soda
½ tsp. salt
1 c. warm water

2 c. flour
1 c. molasses
½ c. melted butter
1 egg

Dissolve baking soda in tbsp. hot water. Put flour, salt, ginger in dish, add liquid and egg. Beat 5 minutes briskly. Place in well buttered loaf pan and bake in moderate oven for 20 minutes.

CRANBERRY PIE

1 ½ c. cranberries
¾ c. raisins
1 tsp. vanilla

¾ c. sugar
2 tbsp. flour
¾ c. water

Put raisins and cranberries through meat chopper, add sugar, flour, water and vanilla. Mix well and let stand.

Prepare pie crust by mixing 1 c. shortening, ½ c. boiling water, ½ tsp. B.P., ½ tsp. salt and 3 c. flour. Roll out thin on floured bread board. (Makes enough for 4 crusts and can be kept for weeks covered in a cool place.)

Cover the bottom of a lightly buttered pie tin with a layer of crust and fill with cranberry filling prepared above. Cover with lattice top crust. Bake in moderate oven until crust is golden.

APPLE PIE

1 c. sugar
1 egg
1 tsp. melted butter

1 ½ c. chopped apples
3 tbsp. lemon juice
grated lemon rind

Mix sugar, well beaten egg, melted butter, lemon juice and a small amount of lemon rind to form a paste. To this add chopped apples and mix so that the apples are well coated. Allow to stand over night. Prepare pie crust as described for cranberry pie and fill with apple filling. Bake in moderate oven until crust is golden.

CHOCOLATE PIE

1 c. sugar	½ c. milk
¼ c. butter	1 ⅓ c. flour
2 eggs	2 tsp. B.P.
1 sq. chocolate	1 tsp. vanilla

Cream butter, sugar, eggs and melted chocolate. Add milk and mix well. Fold in flour after sifting with B.P., and mix well. Fold in vanilla. Split batter between two buttered, round tins and bake in moderate oven. Allow to cool and fill between the two layers with whipped cream or custard. The custard is made as follows: Beat 2 eggs into 1 pt. milk and add 1 c. sugar. Mix well and add ½ c. flour. Cook in double boiler until taste of raw flour is gone. Cool and fold in 1 tsp. of vanilla or lemon extract.

BOSTON CREAM PIE

2 eggs	1 tsp. baking soda
1 c. sugar	2 tsp. cream of tartar
½ c. butter	1 pinch salt
⅔ c. milk	2 ½ c. flour

Cream eggs, sugar, butter and cream of tartar. Add milk and mix well. Fold in flour after sifting with baking soda and salt. Pour batter into 2 buttered, round tins and bake in moderate oven. Allow to cool and fill between layers with custard described above. Cover entire cream pie with chocolate frosting made from 2 sqs. of melted chocolate (in double boiler), 1 tbsp. butter and ½ c. milk. Cook mixture until it just begins to thicken and then remove from heat and allow to cool to room temperature. Add confectioners' sugar until thick enough to spread. Fold in 1 tsp. vanilla.

PLAIN LEMON PIE

1 lemon

1 c. sugar

butter

1 tbsp. cornstarch

2 eggs

1 c. boiling water

Juice lemon and grate rind. Mix sugar and lemon, add butter. Dissolve cornstarch in enough cold water to make a smooth paste. Stir cornstarch paste into boiling water in a sauce pan, and as soon as it boils up again pour over lemon and sugar mixture. Stir until butter has melted. Add eggs (well beaten) and mix well. Bake between two pie crusts in a hot oven. Use pie crust recipe described for cranberry pie above.

BUTTER SCOTCH PIE

1 c. brown sugar

3 tbsp. flour

2 tbsp. butter

1 tsp. vanilla

1 pinch salt

1 c. milk

2 egg yolks

Mix all ingredients except flour and vanilla, then slowly add flour and cook in a double boiler until taste of raw flour is gone. Remove from heat and fold in vanilla. Pour into a cooked pie shell and cover with meringue made from beaten egg whites and a tsp. of sugar.

RHUBARB PIE

1 c. sugar

2 tbsp. flour

¾ c. water

2 c. chopped rhubarb

1 egg

Stew rhubarb, water and sugar until tender. Add flour and stir until smooth. Let cool and stir in beaten egg yolk. Pour into previously baked pie crust. Top with a meringue of egg white, pinch B.P. and 1 tbsp. of sugar beaten well. Bake in moderate oven until meringue has browned.

AUNT EMILY'S MINCEMEAT

1 c. brown sugar	1 c. chopped meat (beef)
½ c. molasses	3 c. chopped apples
½ c. vinegar	1 juice of lemon
½ c. butter	1 juice of orange
1 c. raisins	1 tsp. cinnamon
1 c. currants	1 tsp. mace
¼ c. citron	½ tsp. clove
1 tbsp. salt	

Cook meat in skillet with 1 c. of water. Coarsely grind cooked meat and mix with 1 c. of the cooked juices. Mix with chopped apples, chopped raisins, chopped citron, currants and remainder of ingredients. Add strong coffee to moisten and cook in a double boiler for several hours. Store refrigerated several days before using as a relish or pie filling.

GREEN TOMATO MINCEMEAT

1 tsp. salt	7 lbs. green tomatoes
1 tsp. clove	2 lbs. brown sugar
2 tsps. cinnamon 1 lb. seedless raisins	
1 tsp. nutmeg	¼ lb. orange peel
½ lb. citron	¼ lb. lemon peel
½ c. suet	½ c. cider vinegar
or butter	

Put tomatoes through meat chopper, drain and pour boiling water twice over them, letting stand 5 minutes each time. Add the other ingredients and cook 2 hour in a double boiler. Allow to sit refrigerated before using as a relish or pie filling.

Provincetown's official town crier, Amos Kubic (1930s)

Going to sea

SEAFOOD

BAKED FISH

Filet fresh sole or haddock. Dip filet in melted butter and roll in bread crumbs that have been seasoned with salt, pepper, sage, parsley and onion juice. Place coated fish in a buttered baking dish and sprinkle with squeezed lemon, few drops of onion juice, melted butter, paprika and chopped parsley. Bake in a hot oven until a delicate brown.

HALIBUT with SAUCE

1 lb. halibut	French dressing
mashed potato	salt
pepper	butter
flour	bread crumbs
egg	

Cut halibut into two filets and cover each with French dressing* and let stand. Drain and spread each filet with mashed potato seasoned with salt, pepper and butter. Put the two filets together to form a sandwich. Dip in well beaten egg and again in a mixture of flour and bread crumbs. Fry in hot, deep fat. Serve with sauce described below:

2 tbsp. butter	2 tbsp. vinegar
2 tbsp. flour	½ tbsp. finely chopped onion
½ c. cream	½ c. fish stock
½ tsp. sugar	1 tbsp. chopped olives

Add flour, fish stock and cream to melted butter. Boil vinegar, onion, sugar for 1 minute and add to fish stock and cream mixture. Add chopped olives. *2 parts olive oil to 1 part wine vinegar, dash of salt and pepper.

The Southward Inn in Orleans (1938)

The Southward Inn was owned and operated by Mr. and Mrs. William Rich. With a spacious and comfortable living room featuring a warm fireplace and a library reading room, the Inn was a quiet and pleasant atmosphere in which guest could enjoy the various seasons of the Cape. During the hunting season a special hot breakfast was served at 4 am to guests wishing to make an early start for the fields and blinds. Lunches were made up for fisherman, beach parties, and other day trips of the guests. Room service 24 hours a day was a special feature appreciated by many. The Orleans Cove, directly across the road from the Inn, was a fine boating and swimming area. The Orleans Beach, which is part of the great Nauset Beach near the Inn, was unsurpassed for surf bathing and surf casting. Striped bass were plentiful.

HOLLANDEN HALIBUT

1 ½ lbs. halbut
3 tbsp. butter
1 onion
3 tbsp. flour

¾ c. buttered bread crumbs
6 slices slat pork
½ bay leaf

Put pork in baking pan and spread sliced onion, bay leaf and halibut on it. Cream butter and flour, and spread on fish. Cover with bread crumbs and small strips of salt pork fat. Bake in hot oven for 1 hour.

SOUTHWARD INN SCALLOPS

Cape Cod Bay scallops, which are caught along the shore in the fall, are delicious when baked. Prepare the scallops first by washing and draining fresh scallops to remove sand. Do not allow scallops to remain in water as they will quickly lose their sweetness. Beat a raw egg and add ½ c. milk, season with salt and pepper. Coat scallops in batter and roll in bread crumbs. For each serving, butter a small baking dish and place 20 breaded scallops in it. Add a dash of paprika and a few pieces of butter. Bake in a very hot oven until scallops sizzle and brown (about 10 minutes). Be careful not to over cook, as they will become tough. Not over-working or over-cooking scallops is the secret to maintaining their flavor.

DEVILED CRAB

1 pt. crab meat
4 tbsp. butter
parsley
salt
pepper
cayenne pepper
Worcestershire

2 c. cream
tobasco
1 tsp. lemon juice
1 tsp. onion juice
1 red pepper
mustard

Mix all ingredients and place mixture in baking dish. Cover with bread crumbs and a few pieces of butter. Bake quickly in hot oven.

CODFISH OMELET

4 egg
1 tbsp. flour
1 c. milk

½ c. shredded cod fish
1 tbsp. butter

Moisten shredded fish in boiling water and squeeze dry. Make a sauce of flour, butter, egg yolks and milk. Mix fish with sauce and fold in egg whites and bake ¼ hour in moderate oven.

ESCALLOPED OYSTERS

1 gt. oysters
1 pt. milk
¼ tsp. salt
¼ tsp. pepper

2 eggs
⅔ c. melted butter
24 common crackers

Roll crackers. Combine ingredients and fold in oysters. Let stand 1 hour and bake for 1 hour in moderate oven.

ESCALLOPED FISH

Boil 3 lbs. haddock with 1 tbsp. vinegar and ½ tsp. salt. Fish should remain firm after cooking. Make a cream sauce from

1 pt. milk
1 onion
2 tbsp. sweet pepper
½ tsp. salt

½ c. grated cheese
butter
paprika
2 tbsp. flour

Mix sauce ingredients and cook well in sauce pan. Fold in fish flakes and bake in scallop shells with bread crumbs and lemon juice sprinkled on top. Bake quickly in hot oven. Garnish with parsley and serve hot.

PEPPERS with CRAB MEAT

6 green peppers
6 oz. crab meat
3 tbsp. bread crumbs
pepper

1 onion
2 tbsp. butter
salt

Remove stem and clean out center of peppers. Parboil peppers for 15 minutes. Cook onion with butter, mix with crab meat and bread crumbs. Fill peppers, cover tops with buttered crumbs and bake 20 minutes in hot oven.

FISH TIMBALES

1 tbsp. butter
2 tbsp. flour
½ tsp. lemon juice

2 drops onion juice
½ tsp. salt
cayenne

Mix ingredients and cook in sauce pan with 1 c. milk until thick. Add 1 c. flaked, boiled fish (halibut preferred) and 2 egg yolks (beaten lightly). Fold in well beaten whites of 2 eggs. Put mixture in buttered dish and bake in hot oven ½ hour in pan of water. Serve hot.

BAKED CLAMS

1 gt. clams
butter
2 eggs

1 onion
1 doz. common crackers
1 qt. milk

Rinse, shell and chop clams. Soak in mixture of milk, egg, butter, onion, salt and pepper. Add rolled cracker and blend. Place in buttered baking dish and bake 3 hours in moderate oven.

CLAM CAKES

1 qt. clams
1 egg

1 tbsp. melted butter
2 c. cracker crumbs

Wash, shell and chop clams. Mix alternately with milk and cracker crumbs until easily handled. Add well beaten egg and melted butter. Season with clam juice and pepper. Make cakes the size of fishballs and gently fry in a little butter.

BAKED CLAMS

1 qt. clams

2 eggs

butter

1 onion

1 doz. common crackers

1 qt. milk

Chop onion and clams, and roll crackers. Mix all ingredients together and allow to stand several hours. Place in buttered baking dish, cover and bake 3 hours in moderate oven.

CLAM FRITTERS

1 pt. clams

2 eggs

⅓ c. milk

2 tsp. B.P.

salt

pepper

1 ½ c. flour

Beat eggs lightly, add milk, flour (which has been sifted with B.P.), salt and pepper. Fold in clams and drop by spoonful into very hot deep fat.

LOBSTER NEWBURG

2 lbs. lobster

½ c. cooking sherry

2 c. thin cream

¼ c. butter

2 tbsp. flour

2 egg yolks

Remove meat from cooked lobster and cut in good size pieces. Melt butter and add paprika and sherry. Fold in lobster meat and cook for a few minutes. Sprinkle with flour and fold together. Beat egg yolks and cream, and add to lobster mixture and blend until smooth while simmering. Cook for about 10 minutes and serve on toast.

COD FISH CAKES

Wash 1 c. of salted codfish in cold water and cut in very small pieces (use scissors). Mix the cut fish with 2 c. of diced raw potato. Cook fish and potatoes in water until potatoes are nearly soft. Drain thoroughly and mash until there are no lumps left. Add ½ tsp. butter, 1 well beaten egg and ¼ tsp. ground pepper. Mix well and press into patties and cook in a frying pan with butter until brown on both sides. Serve hot with tartar sauce or ketchup.

Cape Codders were for centuries children of the sea. The deep blue ocean that surrounds the Cape has dominated its history and left its impact on its people. The course of its history, for example, was determined when the Mayflower in 1620 was forced by the dangers of Pollock Rip shoals to take safe harbor at the tip of Cape Cod and not go on to its original destination south of the Hudson River. More recently, the dangerous waters around the Cape were responsible for motivating the U.S. Army Corps of Engineers to build the Cape Cod Canal (1909 -1914). In spite of the canal, ship wrecks have continued to occur around the Cape. In 1936 the fishing schooner Hesperus out of Glouchester hit a shoal in a storm off Chatham. As the crew abandoned the Hesperus in their dories, the ship in some mysterious way suddenly sounded her whistle and turned about, as if to salute them, before going to the bottom. The the relationship between the people of Cape Cod and its dangerous waters has been captured in the short stories of James W. McCue (*Dangerous Waters,* published by The New England Book Co. in 1952).

The Daniel Webster Inn (1938)

The Daniel Webster Inn was built on the site of the first tavern on the Cape. At this site in 1659, in what is now the town of Sandwich, John Ellis opened the first "Ordinary". In 1694 a new structure was built and expanded in the 1800s into the Daniel Webster Inn.

MEAT

PLYMOUTH SUCCOTASH

6 lbs. fowl	4 qts. hulled white corn
5 lbs. corned beef	1 white turnip
8 potatoes	1 pt. New York pea beans

Cook meat and fowl together the day before. Soak beans over night and cook until soft enough to mash through a sieve. Keep hulled corn warm on back of stove. Remove meat and fowl after cooked to tender. Skim off fat from broth. Pare and cut turnips and potatoes into small pieces. Cook in broth. Add mashed and sieved beans to broth. Add hulled and cooked corn. Put meat back in broth long enough to heat, then remove to a platter; broth should be served from a tureen.

BAKED HAM

Boil sliced ham (2 inches thick) for ½ hour. Put in baking pan and cover with 1 tsp. mustard mixed with sugar and water to form a paste. Pour milk in pan to almost cover top of ham. Bake in moderate oven until tender.

HAM SOUFFLE

1 tbsp. butter	salt
1 c. milk	1 tbsp. flour
1 c. chopped ham	onion
2 eggs	parsley
pepper	

Make white sauce of butter, flour and milk. Cook on low heat until taste of raw flour is gone. Add seasoning, ham and beaten egg yolks, and continue to simmer for a few minutes. When cool, add stiffly beaten egg whites, fold gently and put in buttered pudding dish. Bake in hot oven for 20 minutes.

SWEDISH STEW

2 lbs. beef	nutmeg
1 carrot	pepper
1 onion	1 tbsp. salt
1 c. peas	1 tbsp. vinegar
2 tbsp. tapioca	3 whole cloves

Cut beef in small cubes and put all ingredients in earthen dish. Cover with boiling water and cook for at least 4 hours in a slow oven. Remove from oven, cool and store for several days. Reheat to serve.

ROAST LEG OF LAMB

Mix 1 c. cracker crumbs, 1 tsp. salt, 1/3 tsp. pepper, 1 tsp. poultry seasoning and 1.3 c. boiling water. Add 2 tbsp. bacon drippings and 1 chopped onion. Stuff leg of lamb with mixture. Rub entire surface with 1 tsp. salt, 2 tbsp. bacon drippings, and 2 tbsp. flour that have been creamed together. Roast in hot oven about 2 hours. Serve with a mint sauce made by boiling 1 tbsp. sugar with 3 tbsp. vinegar for 3 minutes. Pour over 3 tbsp. of chopped mint and cover until cold. The longer the sauce stands the better it is.

ROAST TURKEY

Wash turkey with warm water and pat dry with fresh, clean dish towel. Rub entire bird with salt and then with a mixture of 2 parts butter and 1 part flour that have been creamed together. Place in pan that has been dusted with flour. Cook in hot oven for 1/2 hour and then add 1/2 c. water to pan. Reduce heat and cook in moderate oven until done. Baste every 15 minutes with drippings from bottom of pan. Do not cover bird while cooking.

CHICKEN CASSEROLE

Clean and cut up chicken. Sprinkle with salt and dredge with flour. Melt some chicken fat in frying pan and fry each piece of chicken to golden brown. Put in a casserole dish and pour the following sauce and vegetables over the chicken.

Cook ½ carrot and ½ turnip cut in cubes, 1 c. peas, sliced onion in melted chicken fat for 10 minutes. Add 2 tbsp flour, salt and pepper. Bring to a boil with constant stirring.

Cover and bake in moderate oven until tender.

CHICKEN and RICE

1 c. chopped chicken	3 c. chicken stock
3 c. boiled rice	1 onion
1 c. sauce	1 egg
3 crackers	

Grate onion and mix with chicken and stir into cream sauce prepared by cooking 1 tbsp. butter with 1 c. milk and 1 tbsp flour. Beat the egg into this mixture and add finely ground crackers. Season with salt and pepper. Put a layer of boiled rice in bottom of a bread pan and layer chicken in cream sauce on rice. Repeat. Pour 1 c. chicken stock over entire layers. Set the pan into another pan containing water and bake 40 minutes in hot oven. Turn out on a platter and pour chicken stock, thickened with a tbsp. butter and tbsp. flour, over top.

Yarmouth Tavern (1945)

Originally, the Yarmouth Tavern (built 1696) was a stage coach stop when coaches ran between Yarmouth and Provincetown. At that time a packet ship brought passengers from Boston to Yarmouth where the stage coach took them to points further out on the Cape. The coaches were later replaced by steam trains from Boston to Orleans (1864). After the demise of the stage coach the Yarmouth Tavern became the private residence of Rufus Holmes until 1923. In 1925 the Tavern reopened, but closed in 1941 with the out-brake of World War II. In 1945 the Yarmouth Tavern opened again, under the ownership of Nellie Barrington a well known New England figure. The Yarmouth Tavern at Yarmouthport is located on the King's Highway.

PICKLES and PRESERVES

SOUTHWARD INN CRANBERRY SAUCE

Wash 4 c. whole fresh cranberries. Mix cranberries with 3 c. sugar and 2 c. water. Cook very gently in well covered pan over low heat. After berries have ceased to pop remove from heat and let cool with cover in place. Do not stir. Flavor and consistency improve with age. With care the cranberries will be whole, transparent and tender, which gives the best presentation on a holiday table.

SOUTHWARD INN CRANBERRY RELISH

To make cranberry relish, use 3 c. fresh well washed cranberries, 2 c. sugar, 1 apple and 1 orange. Put cranberries through a meat grinder along with entire orange (minus seeds) and apple after skin and core have been removed. Stir in sugar and set aside (cold) for several weeks before serving. It improves with storage.

CRANBERRY CONSERVE

1 ½ qts. cranberries	½ c. seedless raisins
1 orange	1 c. walnut meats
2 lbs. sugar	

Put cranberries, whole orange and raisins through meat grinder. Boil until thick. Put in jelly jars and cover with paraffin. Store for at least a month.

QUICK CRANBERRY JELLY

Cook 2 qts. cranberries in 1 qt. water until soft. Strain and save liquid. Mix equal volumes sugar in strained liquid. Stir well and pour into jelly jars and allow to cool. May be served as soon as jell forms.

CRABAPPLE JELLY

½ pk. crab apples
½ oz. cinnamon stick
sugar

½ oz. mace
½ oz. cloves
vinegar

Cook apples in a mixture of equal parts water and cider vinegar (just enough to cover apples in a sauce pan) with spices (in a cloth bag). Strain and save liquid. To liquid add an equal volume of sugar and boil for 5 minutes. Pour into jelly jars, seal with wax and store cold.

RHUBARB MARMALADE

2 lbs. rhubarb
3 lbs. sugar

2 lemons
½ lb. walnut meat

Cut rhubarb fine, cover with sugar and water and let stand over night. Then boil and add lemon juice and rind (cut fine). Boil until thick. Just before removing from heat add walnuts. Pour into jelly jars, seal with wax and store cold.

WHITE TOMATO MARMALADE

1 qt. sugar
2 lemons

1 qt. white or green tomatoes
2 oranges

Heat tomatoes in a double boiler, then drain for 5 minutes. Return tomatoes to the stove with sugar, lemon juice, orange juice and orange rind (chopped and cooked in water until tender). Simmer mixture until it jells. Pour into jelly jars, seal with wax and store cold. Improves with age.

PICCALILLI

1 pk. green tomatoes	6 green peppers
4 onions	1 cauliflower head
6 red peppers	1 c. salt

Chop tomatoes fine, cut cauliflower into flowerets, and cut all else into small pieces. Mix all with salt and let stand over night. Drain well and add:

2 c. brown sugar	½ pt. white mustard seed
1 tbsp. clove	¼ oz. celery seed
1 tbsp. allspice	3 pts. hot vinegar.

Simmer for 30 minutes. Store cold, improves with time.

CORN RELISH

1 ½ doz. ears corn	1 cabbage
4 onions	⅓ c. salt
1 red pepper	1 qt. vinegar
1 green pepper	

Cut corn from cob, put cabbage through food chopper, cut onion fine and peppers in small pieces. Mix together with salt and vinegar and cook for 15 minutes after it is brought to a boil. Remove from heat and set aside.

Mix 1 qt. vinegar, 2 tbsp. mustard, 3 c. sugar, 1 tsp. tumeric powder and 1 c. sifted flour. Cook this mixture until thick. Add cooked vegetable mixture from above and stir until thoroughly heated. Pour into jelly jars, seal with wax and store. Improves with age.

House of the Blue Blinds (1939)

The House of the Blue Blinds, located at 7 North Street in Plymouth, was an elegant restaurant that opened in 1938 under the direction of John and Constance Kenny. The house was built in 1839 by Dr. James Thacher, a native of Yarmouth and grandson of Anthony Thacher who came from Salisbury, England in 1635. The Thacher House was built on the original grant of land to John Cook, who came to Plymouth with his father on the Mayflower.

CHOWDERS and SOUPS

HOUSE OF THE BLUE BLINDS QUAHAUG CHOWDER

6 potatoes
1 qt. quahaugs*
¼ lb. salt pork
3 tbsp. butter

1 onion
1 qt. milk
1 qt. water

Clean quahaugs (remove eyes) and chop coarsely. Dice potatoes and boil in water ten minutes. Grind salt pork and onion, fry until onion is translucent. Drain fat into potatoes, add chopped quahaugs, and simmer slowly in a sauce pan for one hour. Add milk and butter, season well with pepper and salt to taste. Simmer for 1 hour and set aside overnight in cold. Slowly re-heat when ready to serve. * Quahaug (pronounced kwohog) is the large, tough clam found along the shores of Cap Cod. These are better suited for "clam chowder" than the tender Ipswich clam used in other dishes. The toughness of the quahaug stands up to the storage and re-heating necessary for making good chowder.

FISH CHOWDER

1 onion
1 pt. milk
salt
pepper

3 slices fat pork
1 ½ lbs. fresh haddock
5 potatoes
butter

Fry out fat pork, slice onion and brown in fat. Cover fish well with water and boil about 20 minutes (until fish leaves the bones freely). Drain fish and save liquid. Slice potatoes and boil in liquid from fish. Pick over fish, removing bones and skin. When potatoes are soft, add fish, milk and a piece of butter. Season well with pepper and salt to taste. Serve hot. Can be re-heated.

LOBSTER CHOWDER

4 c. milk	2 lb. whole lobster
3 tbsp. butter	2 common crackers*
1 onion	salt
1 c. water	cayenne

Boil lobster for 10 minutes. Remove meat and cut into medium sized pieces. Scald milk with sliced onion and then remove onion. Add milk to a mixture of butter creamed with crackers. Cook remaining lobster body in just enough cold water to cover it, for 10 minutes. Strain and add liquid to milk mixture, then add lobster meat. Simmer for 1 hour and serve hot. Can be re-heated.

CORN CHOWDER

1 c. whole corn	1 onion
3 potatoes	2 c. milk
1 tbsp. butter	2 slices salt pork

Fry the pork and remove scraps. Transfer to sauce pan and add potatoes cut into small pieces. Add corn , onion, salt and pepper. Cover with boiling water and cook slowly for 30 minutes. Remove the whole onion and add the milk and butter. Simmer for for 30 minutes, then store over night. Re-heat and serve hot.

SNUG HARBOR ONION SOUP

2 c. milk	2 ½ c. sliced onion
1 c. water	2 c. chicken stock
5 tbsp. grated cheese	1 c. evaporated milk

Put onions into 3 qt. sauce pan, add chicken stock and enough water to cover onions. Simmer until onions are tender. Add water as needed to keep onions well covered. Add milk and a pinch of salt, heat to scalding. Serve steaming hot with a tbsp. of grated cheese on top of each serving.

LATE SUMMER TOMATO SOUP

celery   very ripe tomatoes
onions   celery
parsley   bay leaves
cloves   brown sugar
salt   butter
flour

Mix ½ bushels tomatoes, 1 ½ bunches celery, 14 parsley leaves, 14 bay leaves, 21 whole cloves, 7 onions, pinch red pepper, 2 tsp. salt, 1 ½ brown sugar, and cook 3 hours. Strain and save liquid. Cream 2 c. of flour with ¾ lb. butter and add to boiling liquid. Simmer for several hours. Serve hot.

CELERY SOUP

celery   1 pt. milk
1 qt. water   butter
tbsp. flour   salt
pepper

Cut the outside stalks of celery in small pieces, boil until very tender in water. Put celery through sieve. When strained, add hot milk, butter, flour, salt and pepper. Simmer for several hours. Sever hot.

INDIAN SOUP

1 qt. milk   ¾ c. butternut squash
3 tbsp. flour   1 onion
2 tbsp. butter   1 tsp. salt
¼ tsp. celery salt   pepper
1 tsp. sugar

Cook squash and push through sieve, then measure out ¾ c. scalded milk with onion. Remove onion and add milk to squash. Mix in flour, sugar and seasoning. Bring to a boil and simmer for 1 hour. Serve hot or cold.

BAKED BEAN SOUP

3 pts. water
2 tbsp. butter
1 tbsp. flour
salt
pepper

3 c. bake beans
2 onions
2 stalks celery
1 ½ c. stewed tomatoes

Mix beans, onions (diced), celery (diced) and water. Cook until celery is tender. Add tomatoes (drained), Chili sauce, salt and pepper. Serve hot.

TURKEY SOUP

savory
celery
salt
butter

turkey carcass
flour
pepper
sugar

Cook turkey carcass in just enough water to cover, 45 minutes. Add ½ tsp. savory, ½ tsp. salt, ¼ tsp. pepper, 1 tsp. sugar, 1 c. chopped celery and 1 tbsp. butter. Simmer for 30 minutes and then add a little flour to thicken slightly. Simmer another 30 minutes. Serve hot.

Yarmouthport

Yarmouthport was known for its graceful trees which covered peaceful streets, terraced lawns and white houses. A typical Cape Cod town where church suppers during the summer and fall months were an important part of the community.

Harwich Church Spire

"CHURCH SUPPERS"

BOSTON BAKED BEANS

1 pt. pea beans or navy beans	1 tbsp. molasses
½ lb. salt pork	2 tbsp. dark brown sugar
3 onions	1 tsp. ground mustard
½ tbsp. salt	

Wash beans thoroughly and soak over night covered with water. Drain, cover with fresh water and heat slowly to a simmer. Allow to cook until skins burst. Drain and set aside. Scald pork rind and cut partially every inch or so. Place beans in ceramic pot and bury pork in beans with top of pork rind exposed. In a separate container mix salt, molasses, sugar, mustard and two cups of hot water. Heat this mixture to a simmer and pour over beans and pork. Bury onions in top of beans, cover and cook at medium heat for 4 hours. Remove from cooking and store refrigerated overnight. On the day to be served, bake for an additional 4 hours, adding water as needed. During the last hour of cooking remove cover and allow pork rind to brown.

SCALLOPED POTATOES

Put in baking dish alternate layers of raw sliced potatoes with raw sliced onions. On top of each layer place pieces of butter, pinch of salt and a little flour. Then add enough milk to nearly cover. Bake 1 hour in hot oven.

POTATOES DELMONICO

Make a white sauce by scalding 2 c. milk and then adding enough flour to thicken. Then add a ¼ tsp. salt and simmer for 15 minutes. Remove from heat and stir in 1 tbsp. butter and set aside. In a well buttered baking dish, place alternating layers of sliced and diced left-over boiled potatoes, white sauce, and grated Cheddar cheese. Cover with bread crumbs and bake for several hours in a hot oven. Remove cover and let brown on top before serving.

POTATOES with EGG

Prepare a white sauce as above. Cut left-over boiled potatoes and hard boiled eggs in strips. Place alternating layers of potatoes (seasoned with salt and pepper) and eggs in a well buttered baking dish. Pour enough white sauce, thinned with milk, over layers to cover all but the very top. Cover with bread crumbs and bake in hot oven until crumbs are brown.

POTATOES with CARROTS

Mix freshly prepared mashed potatoes with freshly prepared mashed carrots. Add enough butter to allow thorough mixing to a smooth texture. Add salt and pepper to taste and keep hot in covered baking dish. If being kept for along time before serving stir in just enough milk as needed to keep moist.

RED DEVIL

1 ½ cans tomato soup	1 lb. cheddar cheese
1 egg	¼ tsp. mustard
pepper	salt
paprika	Worcestershire sauce

Heat tomato and add grated cheese. When cheese has melted add beaten egg to which has been added mustard, Worcestershire, paprika, salt and pepper (enough to make it snappy). Serve on hot buttered toast.

BAKED STUFFED TOMATOES

Select medium sized firm tomatoes. Wash and remove a thin slice from stem end. Remove seeds and pulp and drain most of the liquid and save. In a bowl, mix bread crumbs with salt, pepper, a few drops onion juice and enough liquid to allow salt and pepper to bind to bread crumbs. Fill tomatoes with this mixture and place a small piece of butter on top. Place stuffed tomatoes on a buttered baking pan and bake for 20 minutes in a hot oven. Serve on buttered toast.

SCALLOPED TOMATOES

Drain liquid from canned tomatoes. Season tomatoes with salt, pepper, onion juice and sugar. Cover bottom of a well buttered baking dish with round cracker crumbs and cover crumbs with seasoned tomatoes. Place a thick layer of cracker crumbs, with several pads of butter, on top and bake in a hot oven until crumbs are brown.

CHICKEN SALAD

2 c. chicken meat	¼ tsp. salt
2 tbsp. gelatin	2 tbsp. lemon juice
2 tbsp water	⅛ tsp. onion extract
¾ c. chicken stock	1 c. heavy cream

Dice chicken. Soak gelatin in water and dissolve in stock. Add salt, lemon juice and onion extract. Add chicken meat and let cool, but not jell. Whip cream and fold into the chicken and gelatin mixture, and fill salad molds. When set, turn out on a bed of crisp red leaf lattice. Fill center with pickled fruit or vegetable of choice.

POTATO SALAD

2 pts. diced beats
½ c. diced olives
2 ½ pts. diced boiled potato

½ c. diced sour pickle
½ c. capers

Mix all ingredients together gently, and then add dressing prepared by creaming yolks of 6 hard boiled eggs with ½ pt. oil and ½ pt. vinegar. To this add 1 tbsp. salt, 2 tbsp. dry mustard and 2 tbsp. ground pepper. Mix well.

CABBAGE SALAD

2 c. chopped cabbage
½ c. stuffed olives
½ c. chopped sweet pickles

1 c. chopped walnut
2 c. chopped celery

Mix all ingredients together gently, and add ¾ c. mayonnaise mixed with 2 tbsp. of liquid from the sweet pickles. Mix gently with salad and chill. Serve on iceberg lattice.

VEGETABLE SALAD

1 c. chopped onion
grated cheese

1 sliced cucumber
½ c. chopped green pepper

Place thinly sliced cucumber on crisp lattice leaves. Sprinkle finely chopped onion and green peppers over the cucumber. Over all dust a tsp. of sharp cheese, grated very finely. Serve with dressing made from 4 tbsp. olive oil, 2 tbsp. wine vinegar, ½ tsp. salt, ¼ tsp. ground pepper, ¼ tsp. sugar and ¼ tsp ground mustard, warm and mix until creamy.

First Train From Boston to Orleans (1864)

Hyannis Railroad Station (Late 1800s)

Harwichport Harbor in the Early 1900s

Original Theater of "The Provincetown Art Players"

Hyannis Harbor in the Early 1900s

The Shore in the Late 1930s

Edaville Railroad on the Atwood Cranberry Plantation

The Atwood Cranberry Plantation in the Late 1930s

Ellis D. Atwood

Ellis Atwood owned the largest independent cranberry plantation in the United States. His plantation at South Carver, Massachusetts was home to his collection of narrow gage trains, which at the time of this picture, ran on 6 miles of track around the plantation. Today, Edaville Railroad is a major recreation and preservation site. Train rides are open to the public, an event that is particularly wonderful at Thanksgiving and Christmas time.

CAPE COD

In the 1930s, Cape Cod beyond the canal consisted of 16 towns, 143 villages, 1443 miles of paved roads, 586 miles of shore line, 306 miles of recreational beaches, 277 lakes and ponds, 19 lighthouses, 8 lightships, and 12 Coast Guard Stations. The Towns were named:

Mashpee, for the Mashpee Indians;

Falmouth, for the seaport in Cornwall;

Sandwich, for the seaport in Kent;

Barnstable, for Barnstaple on the coast of Devonshire;

Yarmouth, for the seaport in Norfolk;

Dennis, for the Rev. Josiah Dennis;

Brewster, for Elder William Brewster of the Mayflower;

Orleans, for the Duke of Orleans;

Harwich, for the English seaport of Harwich;

Truro, for the town of Truro in Cornwall;

Chatham, for the town of Chatham in Kent;

Eastham, for the town of Eastham in England;

Hyannis, for the Indian sachem Iyanough;

Bourne, for Richard Bourne, preacher to the Indians;

Wellfleet, for its oyster beds;

Provincetown, for the Province Lands.

A TRIP TO THE "OUTER CAPE"

The drive from Orleans to Provincetown in the 1930s was one of the most beautiful on the Cape. It was a 'roller-coaster' ride which went through 28 miles with quiet and quaint towns of antiquated houses and narrow streets. From the tops of the hills there were the views of Cape Cod Bay to one side and the Atlantic Ocean to the other, and Pilgrim Monument as the constant marker in the distance. The road finally ended in the little fishing village of Provincetown, where the Pilgrims first landed.

A short distance out of Orleans, on the journey to Provincetown, you passed through Eastham, where the Pilgrims first encountered Indians in 1620. Here, in what had been called Nauset, was the home of Aspinet, chief of the Nauset Indians. It was here that John Billington as a child had been taken by Indians and later returned unharmed to the Pilgrim colony.

On approaching Provincetown the journey took you through Truro where the Pilgrims first found drinking water on American soil, and where at "Corn Hill" they first encountered Indian corn.

On arrival in Provincetown, your adventure to the "Outer Cape" began with the studios, shops and theater created by artists, writers and players that stood in strange contrast to the homely simplicity of a Cape Cod seafaring village.

Fishing for Cod, that mainstay of food for all seasons on the Cape, was the most important activity of Provincetown. Boats would sail from Provincetown to the Grand Banks in April and May, carrying dry salt in which they would dress the fish until they returned to the village in September. The largest fare of Codfish ever brought into Provincetown was in 1882 on the schooner Willie A. McKay, skippered by Captain Angus McKay. The boat was out for 3 months and brought back 4,062 quintals of salt dried fish that sold for $22,000!

By 1930 there was only one fishing schooner surviving from the old Provincetown fleet, the schooner Mary P. Gaulart. But many varieties of fish remained plentiful in the waters around the Cape; herring, mackerel, whiting, flounder, butterfish and tuna among them.

Old Flushing Mill Pond in Brewster (1940)

ORLEANS

Orleans is the only town on Cape Cod that has not taken an English or Indian name. In 1792 the Duke of Orleans was in high favor and a visitor to America, and in honor of the Duke the new town took his name. Before then, Orleans had been a part of Eastham.

A great deal of history has taken shape at Orleans, Cape Cod. For example, during the War of 1812 Orleans was frequently raided by British ships based at Provincetown. To escape the dangers of those raids the towns people devised means to dodge back and forth between the Bay and Ocean sides of the Cape. A narrow canal was dug between Boat Meadow Creek on the Bay side to Town Cove on the Ocean side. This canal, known at Jeremiah's Gutter, was the first Cape Cod Canal!

From Orleans one traveled on to Plymouth on the old Kings Highway. The King's Highway runs through a number of delightful old towns. Among the nicest is Brewster, the town next door. This quiet town with enormous elm trees and stately sea captain's homes survives as a lasting tribute to the beauty and graciousness of the Cape Cod experience. Brewster was always known for being the home of more deep water sea captains than any other town on the Cape. Brewster was also the home of Joe Lincoln, Cape Cod's best known author during the 1930s. His first book, "Cape Cod Ballads", appeared in 1902, and 46 novels later, on September 30, 1941, he was honored at the Copley Plaza in Boston by the Governors of New England for his work. Joe Lincoln was the mentor of Jim McCue, who grew up in Orleans.

NOTES

INDEX

Biscuits
        baking powder, 6
        cinnamon, 2
        orange, 9
        parker house, 3
        pop over, 5
        quick, 2
        scotch, 3
        yorkshire, 6

Bread
        brown, 5
        corn, 4,6
        graham, 7
        indian, 1
        nut, 2
        peanut butter, 7
        raisin, 7
        sour milk, 6
        white, 1

Cake
        apple, sliced, 24
        apple sauce, 24
        bread, 8
        buckwheat, 8
        christmas, 24
        coffee fruit, 23
        doughnut, 25
        economy, 21
        huckleberry, 9, 22
        orange, 20
        pancakes, 8
        pound, 21
        salt pork, 22
        sour milk, 23
        sponge, 20
        swampscott, 22
        tea, 21
        union, 23
        waffles, 9

Seafood

Soup

Vegetables